A Little Bit of Dis
   And
      A Little Bit of Dat

A Little Bit of Dis And A Little Bit of Dat

Barbara Hines Gamble

AuthorHouse™ LLC
1663 Liberty Drive
Bloomington, IN 47403
www.authorhouse.com
Phone: 1-800-839-8640

© 2014 Barbara Hines Gamble. All rights reserved.

No part of this book may be reproduced, stored in a retrieval system, or transmitted by any means without the written permission of the author.

Published by AuthorHouse 07/08/2014

ISBN: 978-1-4670-3804-1 (sc)
ISBN: 978-1-4670-3803-4 (hc)
ISBN: 978-1-4670-3802-7 (e)

Library of Congress Control Number: 2011917135

Any people depicted in stock imagery provided by Thinkstock are models, and such images are being used for illustrative purposes only.
Certain stock imagery © Thinkstock.

This book is printed on acid-free paper.

Because of the dynamic nature of the Internet, any web addresses or links contained in this book may have changed since publication and may no longer be valid. The views expressed in this work are solely those of the author and do not necessarily reflect the views of the publisher, and the publisher hereby disclaims any responsibility for them.

Contents

Acknowledgements ix

It's Too Late 1
It's Too Late 3
Trouble Don't Last Always 5
It's Just Who I Am 6
Where, Why, What, and Who I Am 7
Ask 9
Teardrops 10
No Pay, No Stay 12
Advice for a Friend 13
It's A-Coming 14
Say No 15
Excuses 16
I'm Human like You 17
The Churches 18
Food and the One-Time Request 19
Be Yourself 21
Stop 22
The Day Lie Went to Jail 23
The Fighting Couple 24
Access Denied 26
Tomorrow 27
Tomorrow 28
Seasons 29
The Book 30
Politeness 31
Are You Guilty? 32
Our Mother 33
A New Year 34

Don't Tear Down the Bridge	35
The Ghetto Child	36
It's a Lie	37
Find Your Place	38
Let's Pray	39
Somebody Did Wrong	40
Up Pop the Devil	41
Christmas	42
Dr. King	43
Dr. King	44
Dr. King	45
The Street Committee	46
The Truth about a Lie	48
The Old Landmark	49
Carry the Banner On	50
What's Wrong?	51
Our Family Trip	52
Thunder/Lightning	53
Teardrops from Abuse	54
John Doe	55
No Way	57
Abuse	59
Bow-Wow	60
Touched by an Angel	62
Who Called You?	63
Young Lady, You Are Special	64
Blessings	65
A Day with Jesus	66
A Mother's Determination	67
Only the Strong Can Survive	68
Misled	69
Jesus	71
Welcome Home	72
Reflections	73
God Bless Our Troops	74
Men	75
Young Man	76

When the Prostitute Went to Church 77
On Trial 78
Thank You 79
Who's There? 80
Where to Find 81
News Break 82
I'll Rescue Them 83
Too Lame 84
What Is a Home 85
Give Now 86
Sagging Pants 87
Come Together, Let's Pray 88
Prayer for Mankind 89
These Women, These Sisters 90
How Do You Get From Here To There? 91
Little Girl 92
Where Are You? 93
Adams' Chapel 95
Mother Heath 96
Real Talk 97
Looking for Jesus in All the Wrong Places 98
"Thank You, Mom" 99
Take a Look in the Book and See If My Name Is There 100
Do the Right Thing 102
Life 103
Fight On 104
Educate Your Own Child 105
All in Your Smile 107
Watch Yourself 108
Happy Birthday 109
Mess 110
In My House 111
Children Abused by Parents 112
Abuse 113
Abuse Hurts 114
Go Fast 115
Drama Queen 116

A Virtuous Woman of God 117
Christians, Stop Praising the Devil 118
That Young Lady Did Well 119
Thank You, Mom..120
A Gamble Moment of Truth 121
God's Glory..122
Precious...124
Injustice 127
Goodbye, My Love..129
The Godfather of Soul 131

About the Author 133
About the book 135

Acknowledgements

I thank God for allowing me to pursue my dream of being published today after many years of writing, all because my son, Marcus, kept searching until he found someone willing to help and provide information that placed me where I needed to be. Thank you, Marcus, I shall never forget your acts of kindness.

To Virgil, Tiffany, Marcus, Terry, Roi, Lucious III, Dominique, Tyra Mariah, and Virgil Jr., my grandbabies, I love you and I'm grateful for you all being a part of my life. To my friend, Learia Dean Vaughan, thanks for pushing me.

To Lucious Gamble Jr., my husband, a.k.a. Mr. Bug, this is the beginning of something good. Open the door, baby, and let's allow God to take us there together.

To my brothers and sisters, nephews, nieces, other relatives, and friends, thank you for all that you have done. Thanks for words of encouragement that kept me going forward when it seemed so impossible.

To Mrs. Eunice P. Mack and Miss Patricia B. Washington, who worked long hours with me to get this book done, thanks a million! I could not have done this without you.

Finally, I would like to acknowledge three pastors for words of inspiration and prayers:
Elder Patrick Wilson of New Birth Christian Ministries
Pastor James O. Nelson of Eden Baptist Church
Pastor Angela C. Harden of New Destiny Ministries

Each one of you has encouraged and prayed for me that I may be successful in every aspect of life as I go forth and fulfill my purpose.

Theresa, words cannot express the joy I feel and the love I have for you. Thank you for helping to get my work out there. I pray that as you continue to write, God will continue to endow you with wisdom, and that His blessings will always be with you.

In loving memory of:
    My father, Mr. Charles Hines Sr.
    My mother, Mrs. Della M. Rawls-Hines
    My brothers,
    Mr. Willie A. Hines,
    Mr. Leroy Hines,
    Mr. Turner Hines,
    and my nephew, Mr. Tylance Hines

A day doesn't go by without you all on my mind. The family suffered a great loss, but heaven gained wonderful angels. I'm grateful for the time we spent together. There is laughter and tears shed in mentioning your names.

Heaven gained angels
When you were taken from Earth.
God had a plan for each of you,
For He knew what you were worth.
In order for me to make heaven my home,
I too must prepare,
So that when my journey down here expires,
I can find rest in my savior's care.

It's Too Late
(Mama Knows)

It's too late to study,
It's too late to cry.
I did it to myself
So it's too late to lie.

It's too late to run,
It's too late to hide.
How do I tell my mom
I have a baby growing inside?

It's too late to stay,
It's too late to go.
If I don't tell somebody,
My stomach will begin to show.

I am scared and ashamed
Of what I did.
My clothes are too tight
And my stomach is getting big.
What was I thinking?

I know it was wrong.
Now I'm sitting here
Feeling so alone.

Mom's in the kitchen
With her head in her hand.
I've got to tell her this secret
That I can no longer stand.

Mom, I'm sorry, I didn't mean to hurt you.
Mom! I'm pregnant; please tell me what to do.

The mother reaches for her daughter's hand and pulls her in her arms.
They cry for what seems like an eternity,
And then sit down and discuss what
Hopefully her future will be.

I am glad to my mother
I was able to go.
I'm glad she helped me
Because I really didn't know.
She helped me to raise my baby girl.

I was ashamed of how she was conceived,
But she brought joy into this world for my mom and me.

I wasn't too late
And neither are you.
Just make up in your mind and do
What you know in your heart is true.

It's Too Late

It's too late to turn back
The hands of time.
I did it and I knew
The baby was mine.

It's too late; I ran away.
When she told me she was pregnant,
I didn't have a positive thing to say.
Back then I was headed to a top-notch school.
My future flashed before me,
But I treated her cruel.

Today I'm grown and successful too.
Somehow I feel like a failure
Because of what I didn't do.

Perhaps now would be a good time
For me to return home
To find the child I disowned.

I wonder will the mom
Allow me to see
My flesh and blood that's a part of me?

I don't even know whether it's a boy or a girl.
It's sad; I sought a good time
But wasn't responsible enough to take care of
What I knew was mine.

My parents never knew about their grandchild
Because their only child was loose and wild.

Lord, I did wrong—this I must admit.
If you lead me in the right path,
I promise to make it legit.

Back in my hometown at my parents house,
My dad jokingly asks,
Son, when are you going to get yourself a spouse?

The tears broke that were hidden inside.
My parents tried to console me as I cried
Until to them I could explain.
Once I was able to talk,
I told them everything.

Two years later, I'm a happy man
With my brand new family at my side.
My love is shown to them daily;
It, I will never again hide.

Both of them proudly wear my name.
It was from my youthful ways
That brought forth shame.
And for my actions,
There's no one else to blame.

Today my past is gone,
My future is promising and bright.
I thank God for giving me
A chance to get it right.
I was too late to turn back the hands of time,
But today I'm making a difference
In taking care of what is mine.

(2)

Trouble Don't Last Always

Though your problems seem difficult
And sometimes press you down,
It's not the end of the world
Try to smile instead of frown.

When your nights seems restless
And your heart aches with pain,
Give it all to Jesus;
He'll bring sunshine in the midst of rain.

Look beyond the clouds;
Help is on the way.
Jesus nailed those troubles
To the cross, my Bible says.

Come unto me, ye that are heavy laden;
I'll give you rest.
Sometime these burdens
Are merely a test.

Job had troubles to come on every hand,
But he remembered that God
Was greater than man.

What about the woman with the issue of blood?
And let's not forget Noah;
There must have been trouble through the flood.

We are all faced in life with one problem or another,
But there is consolation in sharing
The burdens of your brother.

Tackle those problems by whispering a prayer each day.
Keep the faith and keep in mind
That trouble don't last always.

It's Just Who I Am

I am who I am,
I am not afraid.
I am who I am,
Up and down the streets I'll parade.
I am stepped on and kicked around;
I'm found on every job and on the ground.
I am who I am,
Often causing a stink.
I can tell you
A lie so smooth I won't even blink.
I can and I will
Always be at my best.
Make no mistake about it
For I am known as a mess.

Where, Why, What, and Who I Am

Who am I?
I am what I am,
I cannot deny.
I am what I am;
Sometimes after I try.
I am what some confess
Their lives to be;
I am what in others
They pretend not to see.
I am what in homes
Causes a war.
I am a traveler
From near and far.
I am there in church
With a spare.
I am there to be seen;
I really don't care.
I am the one
Who shows up in
My Sunday best.
I am here so
That you will
Give my phone a rest.
I am what's put on the table
In a rush to eat.
I am what
One looks like
Without the proper amount of sleep.
I am what you look like
When you are knocked down.
I am what you walk into
When caught
Sleeping around.

I am what folks
Many times step in.
Me,
I was invited by a so-called friend.
I am always there
Upon request.
I am here to stay
'Cause
My name is Mess.

Ask

Ask and it shall be given unto you.
Confess your faults, be there many or few.
If you live right and pray,
You can ask for what you will or may.

It makes no difference what the cost;
Jesus is wealthy, there is no loss.
He is a rich and royal King
With a host of angels waiting to sing.

The woman who was sick
Asked to be healed.
The devil asked Jesus
If he could make a deal.

The blind man asked if he could see;
The soldier asked for his child to be free.
The beggar asked for a crumb;
Jesus asks for sinners to come.

Teardrops

The tears she cried
Were tears of joy.
She was thankful the Lord blessed her
With a healthy baby boy.

She gently rubbed
His little nose,
Smiled as she kissed
His fingers and toes.

While she rocked him
In her arms,
She vowed to protect him
From all harm.

She gave her son
That mother's touch,
For in her heart
He meant so much.

As the nurse came
To take him away,
She spoke softly
Please let him stay.

It was at that moment
She prayed for her child.
Lord, I can't thank you enough,
Even though society
Can be cruel and rough.

She watched as the nurse
Took him away,
And she started to weep;
He had brightened her day.
The tears she cried
Were tears of joy.
Again she thanked God
For a healthy baby boy.

No Pay, No Stay

In order to have, one must buy.
To gain success, get up and try.
When a man doesn't work,
He shouldn't be allowed to eat.
Try sitting a lazy man at your table;
Watch him grab first your meat.

We cannot make it
On our feelings alone.
A job is the answer;
Work and bring the money home.

This is the only roof you have
To cover your head,
And if you want to keep it,
For a job you'd better beg.
No pay,
No stay.

Advice for a Friend

If you want to act a monkey,
Go ahead with your show.
But the minute you finish showing your tail,
That's when I'll let you know.
You cannot and will not
With me get your own way.
And during your harsh talk, remember
You too have feelings,
So watch what you say.

What's the use of running
When no one is ever there?
You'd better wise up, my friend,
And get yourself a spare.
Friendship isn't supposed to be abuse;
However, I get the feeling
I'm just being used.
Now, let's hope this little incident
Never occurs again,
Because if it does,
You'll be minus a friend.

It's A-Coming

Yas sir! I sees a better day.
His coming afser while.
If I don't, maybe my chullens
Can run a nusher mile.

Us don board us bird don
In de heat of de day.
Kane Jesus de head Mas sir
Don head us pray.

Us started a long time
In dem cotton fields.
Sanging his be over soon and
Looking to dem hills.

Us couldn't reed,
Sho couldn't rite,
But us got a prayer thru
In da wee ours of de nite.

Yas sar, us barely made hit
On a wang and a prayer,
'Cause us nail-ver four got
Kane Jesus was dare.

Say No

Say no! to drugs, and alcohol too.
Don't bother to explain;
Just speak the words clear and plain.

Drugs do the body harm.
Remove that needle from your arm.
You don't need a joint to pull,
Nor do you need that can of Bull.
Let's get drunk off love and peace
And celebrate with a good clean feast.

Alcohol is poison too.
It effects the minds
Of me and you.
These habits cause one to steal;
If not satisfied, may even kill.

Say no! You won't be a square.
You might be saving
Your own hair.
Just say *no!*

Excuses

Try inviting some folks with you
To the House of the Lord.
You'll find out getting them there
May be rather hard.

We've heard excuses
We thought would never exist.
Have you heard the one
'Bout how I sprang my wrist?
I have a cold and
Cough when I'm too hot.
Just keep on with your lies and
God will know you not.

I don't have a thing to wear and
Could do nothing with my hair
Is what we women say.
The devil sits back and smiles;
You've already made his day.
Our children
We are barely raising
In an environment so strong.
When they make excuses,
We punish them and
They wonder what they've done wrong.

I would've gone to church, but
It was hot (cold) last night.
But that was you I saw
Going in the club, right?
Let whosoever will come and
I'll in no wiles castaway.
If you don't walk in freely,
The undertaker will roll you someday.

I'm Human like You

Don't drive me away
If my clothes are few.
Don't drive me away
If my car isn't new.
People shouldn't be
Chosen by what they wear.
Don't look down on them
For the the style of their hair.

Maybe you have meat
And all I have is bread.
Don't laugh at me;
I'm grateful to be fed.
If you think I'm so dirty
And you say that I smell,
Don't wait till you get in a crowd
To decide you'd like to tell.

You know I'm low on money
And my clothes are few.
Why not look in your closet
And give me one or two?

A coat, some shoes,
All those things I could really use;
And they don't have to be new.
Just don't forget the bridge
That brought you through.

The Churches

We are the churches
Doing right and wrong.
The buildings are the places
Where we pray and sing our songs.

Each day we show our love for God
By the way we treat others.
That's odd,
You say,
You love the man
But
Keep confusion on
The other hand.
Which man do you know?
If you don't stop this foolishness
To hell you will go.

We talk about the Baptist,
Find fault in what they do.
The Methodist is no better,
We talk about them too.
Those sanctified folk,
We scandalize their name.
We church folks
Ought to be ashamed.
We'll get upset
When in church
We can't get our way;
We involve the lawmen
Instead of coming together to pray.

We are the ones who need to get it right.
It's the church folks
That fuss and fight.

Food and the One-Time Request

I love ice cream; I'm crazy about cake.
I love for a good meal to be handed to me on a plate.

If I'm invited to dinner, show me first my seat;
You can pass all the vegetables you like, but don't forget that meat.

Don't give me a beverage, wait until I'm through.
Pass me the rice and gravy, and more of that chicken too.

I am a bit old-fashioned, and I do love my bread,
But if you pass those candied yams, I'll eat them instead.

If you pass me the roast, I need them cabbage too.
What's in that bowl, chile? You better turn it loose.

Once I get up in the morning for breakfast, I love bacon and eggs,
But if you're making biscuits or pancakes, I'll eat them instead.

If you are serving sausage, please let them be beef
'Cause pork upsets my stomach and gets stuck between my teeth.

Don't worry 'bout no lunch, I'll be heading back home.
Chile, you know you outdone yourself; next time I can't come alone.

Just wait till I tell everybody, you know how to treat your guests.
You waited on me hand and foot, and wouldn't let me clean up my mess
I'll take two big slices of cake, and I'll take one of them whole pies, please.

Lord knows I ought to be ashamed of myself cause while I was here
All I did was grease, greased my face to everything that you cooked.
I should've brought my camera and pictures of it all took.

Give me a big glass of tea and a hug before I go.
Lord, I ain't sharing this with nobody;
I'm hiding it in the bottom of my freezer
Where nobody but me will know.

Be Yourself

Don't pretend to be a hammer
When you really are a nail.
Each is of importance
And they both will sell.

A hammer is a strong weapon,
But when polished, the nail will shine.
Don't pretend to be something you're not;
Continue to be humble and kind.

Don't pretend to be a hero
When you know you're afraid.
It's alright to flee
When it involves a gun or a blade.

Be yourself,
Don't live a lie.
One day we all must die.
You may fool man,
But God knows the truth.

Stop

It's high time you and I
Stop pointing fingers at each other.
Don't you know, we should act
Like Christian sisters and brothers?

How can two walk together unless they agree?
Stop talking bad about each other;
Go down on bended knee.

Stop trying to be the ones
To spread bad news.
Stop acting like you are the only one to be abused.
Stop running around doing things
Because you say you're grown.
Stop being a home-wrecker
When you know that is wrong.

The Day Lie Went to Jail

Lie was arrested and hauled off to jail.
It stayed a couple of days
Until it could make bail.
Once placed in a cell alone,
From behind its bars
It began transporting bones.
Lie stated the arresting officer
Gave him a beat-down;
While he was wearing handcuffs,
His face was smashed into the ground.
It couldn't get no one to listen to its lie.

Lie decided it would spice it up
And come back for another try.
This time she served her purpose
With her carefully thought up plan,
Proudly watched from her bunk
While others incarcerated
Began to make all sorts of demands.
No one will ever forget the day
Lie went to jail.
It was a day of turmoil;
It was a day of hell.
Lie bragged about how it was released,
Set free without a fine.
Started the minute that
Satan walked in,
He blew the judge's mind.
Case dismissed.

The Fighting Couple

Every weekend this couple would put on a show;
After taking in too many drinks,
At each other they would give it a go.
They fought in the clubs and out on the streets.
They would be too intoxicated to stand on their own two feet.

After using a few choice words and trying to throw some swings,
They would stumble into their home
On each other laying the blame.

Neighbors would gather around
But no one offered to help;
They would be too busy
Egging them on.
Others laughed while sitting on their doorstep,
But there was an old church mother
Who lingered before God in prayer.

After the crowd disbursed,
She would go over there.
She gave them black coffee and then put them to bed.
She took care of their bruises
And from their Bible she read.

She kissed their foreheads
Before she would leave.
She always prayed to God
That His love they'd receive.

She would turn off the lights
Before leaving, check the stove.
After they were safe and sound asleep,
She would lock the door.

This elderly church mother
Did for others whatever she could.
She was a faithful warrior
Who believed God chose her to do good.

Then one day, God called this woman
From earth to a better home.
And from the legacy she left,
The fighting couple was the pair
Who carried the banner on.

They realized they had lost a dear friend.
It was through her prayers and acts of love
That they accepted Jesus
And lived free from sin.

The prayers of the righteous availeth much.
We never know who in life
Through us will be touched.

Access Denied

Satan, your access was denied in heaven a long time ago;
You admitted to God about Job that you were just walking to and fro.
You cost Adam and Eve their home in the garden.
God used Moses and Aaron to speak to Pharaoh
And you caused his heart to be hardened.

You were to blame for Sodom and Gomorrah's destruction,
And their city filled with sin. You came with homosexuality
And men began lusting after men.

We are tired of all the discord you have sown.
We want our children, spouses, jobs, love, and homes back;
And, Satan, we want you gone.

The only thing about you is, you never stop to rest.
You are known for departing
After you've created a mess.

In the White House courts,
Among countries and nations,
You weren't content
Unless you caused devastation.

You are not welcome.
We demand that you leave.
Too many family hearts
Are left to grieve.

Over and over again you have lied.
We have joined forces against you
To let you know:
Satan! Your access has been denied.

Tomorrow

Take no thought of tomorrow
For thy knoweth not
What a day it may bring. Lift up your head,
Don't be mislead,
Rejoice today and sing.
Consider the lilies of the fields,
How they bloom.
They too are his,
Even the birds are too.
If they take no thought of tomorrow,
Tell me, why do you?

Tomorrow

There's another day
Called tomorrow.
Whether it will bring
Joy or sorrow,
I can't say.
I'm scratching
My head,
Gritting my teeth,
Trying to get through today.

Seasons

What are seasons?
Changes that occur
No matter what the reason.
It's a time, a purpose
For someone or something.
There is a need—
Seasons produce changes.
Some
Cause you to succeed.
Four seasons:
Winter, Spring
Summer, Fall.
To season with spices
That are placed on kitchen walls
Adds savory flavor
And
Changes the taste of food
From plain and simple
To delicious and good.
I've reached a season
In my life
Where I can feel I'm at
My best.
Therefore,
I am stepping forward
Asking Christ to grant
My request.
I know one day
This too shall pass,
But
Right now, I'll make
It last.
Why?
Because it's my season.

The Book

The Bible is our daily guide,
One should read it with joy and pride.
Abraham was the father of the nation,
Jesus offered to all salvation.
Daniel was an interpreter,
Jesus is our mediator.
David prayed to God for help.
Jesus's love for Lazarus states in
John 3:16 that he wept.
Nicodemus came to Jesus by night
Asking questions about how to get his soul right.
Two men went up into the temple to pray;
They met a lame man along the way
Who was begging for silver and gold.
When Peter asked him,
Wilt thou be made whole?
Remove your Bible from the shelf.
Pray for understanding
As you read it for yourself.
Find out how the world began
And what will happen before it ends.

Politeness

Please and *thank you* are the polite words to say.
Yes, sir and *no, sir* will take you a long way.
It's not going to hurt you to give others respect—
It just goes to show teaching you didn't neglect.

Yeah and *naw* aren't good grammar at all.
Fancy words you don't have to use,
But politeness is the tool.

Are You Guilty?

As I was walking down the road,
I met a man struggling with a load.
I moved to the other side.
Me! Helping that old dirty man—
I have so much pride,
I turned up my nose,
For he had such an awful smell.
With my head held high
I tripped on something and fell.
He slowly dragged over to me
And extended his hand.
I was shocked, jumped up and thought,
The nerve of that old man!
Come that night as I began to pray,
I heard a voice say,
Pause, hypocrite, before you pray.
I sent someone to you today.
To whom have you reached out?
Your heart could use a good transplant;
The good you do for others
Can be measured by the size of an ant.
Your values are flowing with streams of hate.
Change your ways before it's too late.
You've walked in darkness too long.
Your deeds are sinful and in hell you will roam,
If you don't change your ways.

Our Mother

By
Bernese and Barbara Hines

Some years ago our mother died.
Everyone who knew her knows she really tried.
She was a wonderful mother,
A friend to one and all.
She did her very best
In situations great and small.

If tears could bring her back
She'd be with us today,
But God saw fit
To take our mother away.

She has left us now,
But with a job well done.
No one can take your place, Mother,
No, not one.

A New Year

5-4-3-2-1,
A new year has begun.
Tell me, what will you do?
Make resolutions that just aren't true?
Promising to stay home more, why now?
Are you watching the door? You say
You're going to talk less.
Well, that's good,
Your mouth could use a good rest.

5-4-3-2-1,
Ring in the New Year.
Are you going to have fun?
One night out really won't hurt.
Look at your clothes
Covered in dirt.

Learn some sense and fast—
All that partying
Isn't going to last.

Go to church, learn to pray.
Ask the Master to teach you His way.
Don't drink and drive—
There are others that would like to survive.

Let's not forget about crack—
It is a bad attack.
Leave all that junk alone.
Wise up and run on home.

Don't Tear Down the Bridge

Just because success
Has become a part of your name,
Don't tear down the bridge;
You'll need it just the same.

Didn't that bridge bring you
Across many days?
Don't get a big head
And start changing your ways.

Don't start putting me down
Because of your new car.
I remember a long time ago
You drank water from a jelly jar.

You know we were neighbors
From way back then.
I wish you good luck,
But you're going to need a friend.

An airplane flies so high
Before it comes back down.
If you get too high and fall,
You'll be the talk of the town.

The Ghetto Child

The ghetto child struggles awhile,
Searching hard to learn,
Knowing without a good education, money is hard to earn.
Many times they are
Abusively cast aside
But
Have to swallow pride
Or else give up hope.
If the determination
Is sincere,
Must be misled with
Dope.
Wearing the same
Old pair of shoes
Walking down that
Dusty road,
Transferred to many schools.
Many days the meals
Were few, but
Begged for something
Until a job came through.
The ghetto child
Did succeed.
Now I bid you,
Stop and take heed.

It's a Lie

Some folks lie for fortune and fame,
Some can't help it; it's a part of their name.
A lie is seldom told the same;
It doesn't care on whom it pins the blame.
A lie started a long time ago, and since the beginning,
It continued to grow.
Lies have caused many to go astray,
It's like wildfire that's out of control today.
A lie is told in many forms and fashion;
Its sole purpose is to use as a tongue-lashing.
Some say I did it so you would be spared;
The truth would have showed how much you cared.
A lie when told can sometimes be funny,
But if you want to keep friendship,
Don't lie about money.
Lies that are told between husbands and wives
Have been known to tear up homes and destroy lives.
A lie will never carry its own weight.
It's not reliable; you can't take it on a date.
If you tell one lie, you are bound to tell two;
It becomes a habit that sticks with you.
A lie has never held a job,
But from it, many employees were robbed.
A lie has never attended school
But was there by the people it used.
Even when it went to jail,
It falsified documents
About how in trouble it fell.
Stating the trouble was never its fault,
Wasn't doing a thing,
Don't know why he was sought.
Lie has a record, a rap sheet long,
Claiming the judge did it wrong,
A lie can be told so smooth;
Watch out or you might be fooled.

Find Your Place

We are on a mission for the King.
All can preach, many can't sing.
Each one of us should get in our proper place.
Do your jobs diligently with a smile on your face.

If it's your job to usher, stand there and do it well.
Don't try to please your fellow man;
Out of anger, they may tell.

Maybe you're a deacon that can pray a prayer good.
One other thing required:
Live the life that you should.

Walk upright before the youth.
Not an eye for an eye
Nor a tooth for a tooth.

Come along, choir members,
Give a selection or two.
Don't put on airs
Like to you this is new.

Open your mouth and sing
One of the well-known hymns.
If you don't know them,
Sing, "Fill my cup to the rim."

We are daily walking by faith;
Get in a hurry and find your place.

Let's Pray

You pray for me;
It's the right thing to do.
I want you to pray
Only if you can get through.

It's okay for us
To come together and pray for rain.
Lord knows we need it
To help the grain.
But let's pray
For that someone who's lost,
Who may not realize
Jesus paid the cost.

Somebody Did Wrong

Adam and Eve were placed in the garden
With only one command:
On the tree in the midst of the garden,
Do not lay a hand.
Adam gave every animal the Lord
Formed, a name.
Sounds like a genius
With a magnificent brain.
These two people didn't abide
In the garden for long.
They were strongly persuaded
And for them things went wrong.
The serpent came along one day
With a plan he had laid:
Ah, Eve! About that tree over there…
What a command the Lord gave.
After fixing his lie so smooth,
He knew he had those two fooled.
They realized
They were naked yet
No one had told them so.
The devil, pleased
With himself,
Said, *It's now my time to go.*
There was a man
Named Samson
Who fell in the very same snare
By revealing to Delilah
His strength was in his hair.
These men claim to have
Been so smart.
Better stand up strong
Before something like
This happens again and
Causes all to go wrong.

Up Pop the Devil

I heard this sermon
One Friday night,
About how Satan
Tries to start a fight.
As funny as this may seem,
Up pop the devil
With all of his schemes.
When you are determined to do your best,
Up pop the devil
To try and make a mess.
He's no easy quitter,
Deals directly with the mind;
Proudly sits back and smiles
When peace you cannot find.
Uses both the young and old,
Working overtime to destroy their souls.
When the churches are progressing along,
Up pop the devil and things will go wrong.
He'll walk in to let you know he's there;
If you aren't prayerful,
He'll bring along a spare.
In the choir he sings so loud,
Makes you think the angels are floating on a cloud.
Resist the devil,
And he will flee.
In order to do that,
Go down on bended knee.
God is able to see you through,
But say get back, Satan,
I want no part of you.

Christmas

Christmas is a time of joy
For every little girl and boy.
Christ was born on Christmas day,
Is what the older people say.

Dr. King

Dr. Martin Luther King, Jr. marched here and there;
Every now and then, he whispered a prayer.
He marched for all mankind to see
That people everywhere want to be free.
Dr. King had a dream about you and I,
That one day hatred and prejudice would die.
This great man gave us the right to vote,
And he fought for others, this I quote:
"We shall overcome." As we walk this life,
We must overcome some envy and strife.
Man everywhere should have freedom of speech;
Blacks, too, are now qualified to teach.
Dr. King since then has passed away;
So you see, he has brightened our day.
Let's join hands with each other
And walk the land as sisters and brothers.

Dr. King
(The Dreamer)

Dr. Martin Luther King, Jr. walked the dust.
He met all kinds of people
Who kept up fuss.
He kept marching and trusting in the Lord,
Knowing the task at hand would be hard.

Let freedom ring
Across the land.
God showed me a dream
And I have a plan.

A man shouldn't be judged
By the color of his skin.
God created us all from Adam—
Shouldn't that make us kin?

Let truth, loyalty, and justice abide;
Away with hatred, prejudice, and pride.
I have a dream that time will pass
And mankind everywhere will be free at last.

Dr. King
(A Nonviolent Man)

Dr. Martin Luther King, Jr.,
A nonviolent man,
Tried to establish integration
All across the land.

It makes no difference
Where you're from;
People as a whole
Should be accepted as one.

Away with mobs and the Klan too.
Accept me for who I am,
And I'll accept you.

He led the march but was never alone;
There were many others
Who left their homes.

I saw the promised land
and was much pleased.
It was so beautiful,
It put my mind at ease.

We didn't march to gain fortune or fame;
We fought for freedom and for a change.
Dr. King died a happy man;
He fulfilled his purpose to lend a hand.

After closing his eyes,
At the setting of the sun,
The thought, *We have fought for justice*
But the battle is not won.
Mankind everywhere should be accepted as one.

The Street Committee

They are in every town, city, and state,
Roaming from house to house
With gossip and hate.
They are the ones who invite themselves in,
Professing that they want to be your neighborhood friend.

They are small in number,
Claiming they came over to help.
The street committee is full of troublemakers
Climbing up your doorstep.

My advice to you is do not let them in.
If you do, that's when your troubles will begin.
They are trying to get in your business
And will bring lunch as an excuse.
Don't get involved; these women are very loose.

They have sincere looks on their faces.
When they think you aren't watching, they scan your place.
They are quick to tell you that since you are new,
It's their job to come and welcome you.

They will inform you not to hesitate to call,
And then they introduce themselves
while waiting for you to tell it all.

There is usually one that will lead the pack—
She does all the talking as the others stand back.
Once they have learned things about you,
They make a quick getaway, declaring they have things to do.

Remember that they offered to help, but never once did they lend a hand;
The purpose of their visit was to see if you had a man.
They want to know if you have money
So from you they can bleed.
Watch out, people, the street committee is a dangerous creed.

Give them a day or two, and they will want no part of you.
They are seeking people with weak minds;
Those they can prey upon—
They love that kind.

If by chance you put them in their place,
The language they use is a scandalous disgrace.
They will spread rumors all about you—
How you tried to come between them too.

They keep up confusion on every hand;
The street committee I can't stand.
In their eyes, others are always wrong.

They are soliciting members
So they can be strong.
The catch is you join for a small fee—
Either money or use of your car for free.

They love to borrow
But will never repay.
If you see the street committee,
Go the other way.

None of them can keep a man,
But they are willing to destroy
Every home that they can.

The Truth about a Lie

Daddy planted it, Mama conceived;
The doctor delivered Satan's seed.
When they were born,
They came in a pair,
So that when one grew weary,
There was always a spare.
When the cords were cut, the damage was done;
It was like an electric shock that left the doctor stunned.
Lie and Liar were wrapped in a blanket to keep them warm
And placed in an incubator to be protected from harm.
When they were held for the very first time,
It was googie—sort of like slime.
Somehow they attacked the hearts of women and men;
From that brought forth sin.
Satan used them as he tricked Eve.
Eve used them and Adam believed.
Lie gets up each morning with its ugly head held high,
Searching through the newspapers to see who it can fry.
It has many gadgets that are often used
To discredit mankind and keep them confused.
Lie has walked past churches and schools but never attended,
Didn't stay long enough for truth to sink in.
It claimed to have graduated with honors and many degrees
But never produced certificates
For the family to see.
Finally Lie confessed it needed religion;
Shuffled some cards and made a swift decision.
It went from one denomination to another,
Transforming the hearts of sisters and brothers.
But stating that religion stuff was a bit too strong,
Decided to leave it alone until the church folk did wrong.
The truth about a lie
Is that it will not last—
Although it has been known
To travel fast.

The Old Landmark

Let's go back to the old landmark
Where parents were much concerned.
Turn the pages slowly,
From them a lesson can be learned.
Children then were responsible
And honest too;
When adults spoke they listened
And did as told to do.
It made no difference whether
You were their child.
If told to sit there,
You did so with a smile.

Crimes were low
And babies were few,
But today unwed teenagers
Are guilty of about two.

Our parents didn't leave work
To run to the schools,
Because whippings were rendered
And we obeyed the rules.

Each teacher had a strap
He often would use.
Today, you have a choice
Of which discipline to choose.

The old landmark
Was strict and tight,
But one thing about it—
It was alright.

Carry the Banner On

The circle is broken,
We have loved ones gone.
We must be survivors,
We must carry the banner on.

Daily we cherish the thoughts of those
Who are in our hearts so deep.
We miss them profoundly;
Often times we weep.

The families are struggling
Just to carry on.
We know our loved ones
Would want us to be strong.

We feel lonely and then we feel glad.
It was a blessing
To have you all in our lives.
Thank you for the good times we had.
Although we are grieving,
We must be strong.
For we are the ones
Who must carry the banner on.

What's Wrong?

What's wrong in our homes?
Our children are spending
Too much time alone.
We understand that
For them you must provide,
But
Who's there
When they need to confide?
What happens
When and if decisions
By them are made?
Can we as parents
Live with the freedom
To them we gave?
What happens when
You realize that your child is grown?
It all came about
When
We, the parents, left them
Too long alone at home.

Our Family Trip

The children were excited, but
So were Mom and Dad,
To be going away on vacation—
It's the first one that they ever had.
Dad made a promise
A long time ago that when we least expected it,
That's when we would go.
It seemed that since Dad joined the church,
We do more things together;
Our weekends are hardly the same.
He sometimes plays catch
With my brother and me.
After we built the girls a dollhouse,
He even sits in there with them
And from their small toy cups pretends to drink tea.
Mom walks around with a smile on her face,
And now before we eat, Dad or one of us says the grace.
As we set out to take our family trip,
Mom packed sandwiches
Fruit, drinks, and dips.
Daddy said a prayer before we entered the van.
We had a great time together
On the family trip that for us our dad had planned.

Thunder/Lightning

It seems so amazing to me
That when it thunders and there's lightning,
How different people can be.
They'll call on the Lord
To help and have mercy, please,
And as soon as the sun comes out
They are back at ease.
Child,
You better sit down and listen
To the Lord speak.
What about His commandments?
Did He not command us them to keep?
If He built the church,
He meant for us to go there;
Through His word He teaches us how to care.
Some people can't tell you
The last time to church
They have been,
But
Let the thunder and lightning
Roar and flash,
Lord! They are quick to confess their sins.
They will put down the bottle
'Cause they don't want lightning to strike.
Soon
As the storm is over,
They're back in the Devil's track.
You'd better stop
Playing with God;
He is a jealous God
Who
Does not like being robbed.

Teardrops from Abuse

Down her cheeks rolled
Tears of pain.
She was tired of fighting
And it left her drained.
She gave all she had,
But to her husband,
It was never enough.
With her, he was always mad
Because his life was rough.
He drank every day a beer or two.
When he started using drugs,
She told him they were through.
She was at the door
Preparing to leave,
When he hit her from behind
And her head began to bleed.
Down on her knees she hit the floor
As he began to beat her some more.
Why? Because he felt like his life was bad
And he grew up without a dad.

John Doe

This is a story about John Doe;
I'd like to share it
Everywhere I go.
The names have been changed
To protect mainly two—
Keep in your mind
It can be me or you.
Poor old John didn't live long;
Died at age thirty-three.
John had a habit,
One he refused to kick.
I caught him using drugs,
He said they made him tick.
There are many people
That have felt the very same way.
Many, like John Doe,
Are not here today.
He had three children;
All were boys.
On Christmas they were sad
'Cause
They never got toys.
Jane worked hard
While John sat at home each day.
Come every Friday,
He went to get her pay.
He wouldn't take it all,
But what he left was much too small.
Yet he complained when they didn't have food.
People, in your minds I'm sure
You thought John was rather rude.
He worked many jobs
That didn't last long.

Each morning he swallowed his thrills,
And that's where John went wrong.
Jane raised the boys
The best that she could.
Told them many stories
About drugs being no good.
I said that just to say this,
In dealing with drugs
It is a bad risk.

No Way

There's no way you will
Hug me and tell me it's alright,
When every weekend
All we do is fight.
There is no way you can look at me
After giving me a black eye.
There's no way
You can comfort me
When you beat me and make me cry.
Why do you want me to stay
When you throw me toward the door?
How can I be your girl one minute,
When the next minute you're telling your friends
I'm nothing but a whore?
Why do you take me out
Just to sit at the table alone,
While you're on the dance floor
Getting your groove on.
When I'm at the table,
The only time you look my way
Is if somebody stops
And/or has something to say.
But as soon as we get home,
You begin to throw a fit.
With your fist closed
My face you start to hit.
I don't know what's the matter with me
To stay and be treated like this.
You promised you would change
When you broke my wrist.
I have had broken bones,
Fractured skull, all that came from you.
The doctors urged me to press charges,

The policeman has told me that too.
You call me names that are of a disgrace.
I will never forget the day
You spit in my face.
You have abused me for
The very last time.
You are a poor excuse for a man,
One who is only good
With his fist, foot, and hand.
I'm tired this time—
I am through.
No matter how much money you have
I want nothing more to do with you.
The policemen are waiting
Outside this door.
If I so much as scream
They'll drop you on the floor.
I am going down to the station
With documents in my hand.
I will be pressing charges
And testifying on the witness stand.
You will be the target,
Labeled as abusive
With low self-esteem,
All because you're a short man
Who gets a thrill by abusing women
But wont stand up to a man.

Abuse

Abuse isn't always done by a man;
There are some women
Who also love to use their hand.
Their tongues are full of deceit,
They have good men in the home,
But love life in the street.
They have a book full of male friends
They hang with all the time.
If he is caught talking to a female,
She acts like he's lost his mind.
Oh, you just wait until
I get you home!
That too is abuse
And it is so very wrong.

Bow-Wow

Why should a man
Act like a dog?
If he must be an animal,
Why not be a frog?
Ribbit, ribbit,
Hop away.
I don't even like the games
You play.
A dog is the lowest thing to be,
And acts so indecently
For everyone to see.
He'll smell Sally
And will play with Sue, and
While both females are watching,
That skunk will
Turn and screw Lou.
Screw her until her tongue hangs out;
And it matters little to him
Whether the others pout.
Some men today are the very same way;
All they want to do
Is run in and play.
But I've got news for you, Mr. Great Dane,
I'm the poodle and I've been trained
Not to let my hair down for you.
I see what the deal is
And I see that you are through.
Your voice is heavy
And your body looks strong,
But here you do not belong.
Now take your bowl as well as your bone,
And find you a sooner 'cause you got me all wrong.
Nothing do you have and nothing will you get;

I don't intend to treat you as a pet.
I refuse to be torn down, especially by you,
Old jive-time clown,
Bow-wow, bow-wow, ruff-ruff.

Touched by an Angel

When my life was full of danger,
God sent me down an angel
To walk me through the storm.
When I felt abandoned and alone,
The angel cradled me
In its protective arms.
There were times I wanted
To run and hide,
But the angel was there as my guide.
Christ promised never to leave us alone;
He sends angels
To comfort and keep us strong.
So be careful how you entertain strangers,
For some have entertained angels unaware
They are there to be a blessing
To you and me,
And God has placed you in their care.

Who Called You?

I called the old
Because they know the way.
They're now having trouble
Trying to obey.
The old are trying
So hard to look new;
With their new attitudes,
How can you tell who's who?
It should be a blessing
To live to grow old.
Stop acting foolish and
Get concerned about your soul.
God, give me strength to accept
The things I can't change.
Women bring down your dresses—
It's alright to look plain.
Teach young women
How to live right,
To love their families,
Don't fuss and fight.
Young people, I call you because
You are strong.
Now I want you to be the ones
To call on.
Feed the flock
As I say do.
Don't sugar coat the gospel,
It needs no help from you.
Stand tall,
Speak firm,
No fancy words, or big terms.
Just remember,
In all you do,
God was the one
You said
Called you.

Young Lady, You Are Special

From the first conversation that we had,
It touched my heart and made me glad.
I could only reminisce in my mind,
That young lady is special,
Someday I'll make her mine.
She has such a pleasant appearance,
Her eyes glow like a light.
It's something special about her;
I don't want her out of my sight.
The charm she has,
I wonder if she knows it's there?
She has touched my heart
And love is in the air.
She carries herself with style and grace,
And when she laughs it drives me wild.
I can't wait for tomorrow to come
So that I can embrace her and let her know
That she's the one.
Sixteen months have passed,
Yet I feel the same—
I want that young lady
To wear my name.
Tonight I'll ask her
To be my wife.
Forty-two years have gone by,
Yet there are still flames.
It's not one-sided;
We both feel the same.
Each day we express
How deeply we care;
We pray together and thank God
For the love that is there.
We have four children
Who are now grown and have moved away from home,
But we are never alone.
Why? Because that young lady is special to me.

Blessings

What are blessings?
A gift from one to another.
Jesus gave His life
For you and my brother.
When they nailed him to the cross
And they hung him high,
He said, "Father, forgive them
For they know not what they do."
If Jesus can give and be a blessing,
Then why can't me and you?
You ought to walk up
To somebody in need and
Bless them like you've lost your mind.
Give it and forget it,
And good fortune will be thine.
Cast thy bread upon the waters
And not many days after,
It shall be returned.
Give willingly and obediently,
For in so doing, a lesson will be learned.

A Day with Jesus

I spent the day with Jesus,
I sat down at His feet.
He placed my head in His lap
As He took His seat.
His lap is very light
As if no body form was there.
My reply was, "Jesus,
You seem so weightless.
On you, can I cast my cares?"
The robe He wore was white,
My tears had left no stain.
When I looked into His fiery eyes,
He removed my aches and pains.
I shook my head that once was filled
With clutter and debris;
In a voice like running water
Jesus said, "Daughter/Son, I've set you free."
He touched my lips with a finger,
Left a burning deep down within.
Again my Savior spoke and said,
"I have forgiven all your sins."
I weakened for a moment,
But later grew powerful and strong.
That left me embracing Jesus;
That's where I felt I belong.
The day I spent with Jesus
Left me feeling fresh and brand new;
If you need a change in your life,
Spend a day with Jesus too.
Your life will never be the same—
All of your worldly ways
Jesus will change.

A Mother's Determination

Hush, little baby, please don't cry—
I know you want and need milk.
All I got is a whole lot of guilt;
I got laid off and my paycheck is already spent.
The landlord threatened to evict us
If I didn't pay the rent.
Hush, little baby, please don't cry—
I've got a little meal;
I'll make you some bread.
Oh God, no!
I can't believe the meal is covered with mold.
I'll go over to Mrs. Jones,
Maybe ten dollars she'll let me hold.
Hush, little baby, please don't cry—
Somebody will help us;
All I need to do is try.
Lord, my life is so hard,
I can really use a hand.
My baby daddy isn't active,
Plus he's a married man.
He told me his house
I was never to call;
Now I'm backed up
Against this brick wall.
And I don't have a clue.
My baby is hungry,
But so am I
Yet I don't know what to do.

Only the Strong Can Survive

There's plenty of work
For us to do;
Let's stand stronger
Than Clorox 2.
We can't be victims of defeat;
We want recognition
For an honorable seat.
In order for us to survive,
We must prove that we're tougher than Tide.
It's been said we don't exist,
But we all know that's a bad risk.
Fellow workers stand up and
Acknowledge your rights.
It's gonna get nasty—
Are you prepared for the fights?
Believe that you hold the key
To the strength you need to set you free.
Inside you there is great power;
Don't take down—
Be a survivor.
Only the strong can survive!

Misled

By false information
Thousands are dead,
So you probably figured
My name is Misled.
I've persuaded many not to pray;
I've convinced the toughest
To walk my way.
I'm never content;
When homes are operating smooth,
I quickly begin
To sharpen my tools.
If I can plant doubt
In one spouse's mind,
I begin to rejoice,
For I know that love is blind.
Winter, spring, summer, or fall,
I work year round with no break at all.
North, south, east, and west,
I've been to those places
And gave it my best.
I've never met a man
That I couldn't change
In one way or another.
In my home I wasn't content
Until I changed the image of my brother.
I strut when I walk
And I do it proud;
I have the assurance,
I'm floating on a cloud.
I fear we haven't met
Face-to-face;
It must be that you
Have God's love and grace.

Even though my name is Misled,
I'll never stand honest
On anything I said.
If you are searching for joy and pride,
Don't be persuaded by such a fast ride.
All of those that enter this race
Must one day meet their maker face-to-face.
Don't be misled.

Jesus

Jesus paid a visit
To this town one day.
He stopped down the road
To call upon a sick man.
Along the way,
There was a family travelling together
Who was almost home.
Jesus called for the parents
And left the children alone.
He visited the hospital but
Didn't inquire of the sick.
He called one of the visitors
And her death was rather quick.
There were some workers
Plowing in the field, but
Jesus chose a little girl
Who was riding her bicycle
Up and down the hill.
He called a lawyer who was preparing for a case.
He called three little children in a wreck
That left one without a face.
You don't have to be sick
Or in any kind of pain,
But you do have to answer
When Jesus calls your name.
Warning signs are flashing and trouble is in the land;
John the Baptist preached, "Repent!
For the time is at hand."
We love our loved ones
And Jesus does too.
So just be ready to answer
When Jesus calls on you.

Welcome Home

If on earth you've labored
Faithfully and your debts are paid in full,
There's a resting place for you
And a crown covered in jewels.
There's a home in glory
Where the streets
Are paved with gold,
With a host of angels welcoming you
And with rest for your weary soul.
The robes worn are white
Without a spot or stain;
Welcome Home is what I want to hear
When Jesus calls my name.
No more pain,
No more sorrow
When there I take my seat.
I will be forever
Sitting at the Master's feet.

Reflections

Someday I hope to be just like my dad.
He was a great provider
And he made sure his family had.
Some day I hope to be
Just like my mom—kind and loving
Never causing harm.
Our parents taught us to stand
For things that were right.
Our mom wasn't one to fuss or fight.
She said to speak the truth and move on,
But you must admit
When you are wrong.
Our dad said to take your punishment like a man;
Always strive to be the best that you can.
They had for their children hopes and dreams;
We were large in numbers
And we all were a team.
They wanted each one of us to succeed;
They made sure we did our homework
And bought books for us to read.
Our parents took us to church
And they taught us to pray.
They taught us how to work
With our own hands
In order to receive an honest pay.
As I stand at the foot of their graves,
I am grateful for the teaching they gave.
As I live, I will continue to be
A light and now a reflection for others to see
That Christ is living in me.

God Bless Our Troops

They're fighting hard
And
They're fighting strong
To
Protect America
From all harm.
God bless our troops.

Men

When it comes down to churches
There's a shortage in men.
That's why we women
Are walking on in.
Now we're not trying to take your places—
Only helping the Pastors
Fill the empty spaces.
God made man;
We know these words are true.
But, Men, wake up and do
What you ought to do.
The harvest is plenteous
And the laborers are few.
God has enough work
For both men and women to do.

Young Man

Young man, please don't let it be too late.
You must stop the violence,
You must stop the hate.
It's sad to see and hear about a young man using a gun.
And it's heartbreaking to hear of them
Shooting and killing for fun.
How can you take a life
That wasn't yours to give?
Who placed the decision in your hands
About who should or shouldn't live?
It's time to break the cycle.
If your family members
Are incarcerated and doing time,
Wise up, young man, reconstruct your mind.
Trouble is easy to get into
And difficult to walk out of.
Money can't buy freedom.
If it could, lots of the problems would be solved.

When the Prostitute Went to Church

The prostitute went to church one Sunday
After working the streets all night.
Once she entered the church
That almost constituted a fight.
The usher at the door
Fell on the floor
Complaining that he couldn't breathe.
He was a regular at her place and was known for doing
With the prostitute whatever he pleased.
As she strutted to the front,
Several other deacons began to grunt.
One deacon was getting ready to raise a hymn,
But one look at the prostitute and he shouted,
"Brother, today our chances are slim!"
Not one of the deacons were willing to pray;
They all seemed to be speechless,
Not knowing what to say.
The speaker was a guest
Who never looked up
from his paper the whole time he read.
The minute he cut his sermon short,
From the pulpit he fled.
The prostitute smiled
Because she had won the game.
When she walked into that church,
Not one person did she have to name.
The guilt on their faces clearly showed the blame.
She vowed someday to return again,
Not to discredit the men,
But to show up those shouting sisters
And to tell where they too had been.

On Trial

I arose this morning hoping to make it
Through the day. I didn't want to be selfish
So I tried to help someone along the way.
First, I was yelled at for no apparent reason.
I simply sucked it up and said
Maybe it's my season.
Then I was cussed at and called everything
But a child of God again.
I smiled and said
I put my trust in you, Lord.
At the end of the day,
I continued to rejoice
Because of my decision
To make Jesus my choice.
No matter what comes your way,
Be encouraged and continue to pray.

Thank You

Thank you for the food we eat;
It is good bread and good meat.
It was prepared with love and care.
Mother this is great; we'd like to share
With those who don't have a bite to eat
And don't know what's like to taste meat.
We are blessed to have a meal
Fixed so nicely by our mother dear.

Who's There?

Who's there for the children?
Who's there to fix the meals?
Who's there to dress them?
Who's there to wipe their tears?
Who's there to teach them right from wrong?
Who's there for them to lean on?
Don't wait until they are grown men,
Before you own them as an heir.
They need you now and you need to be there.

Where to Find

Where to find help in the time of need?
Pick up your Bible and begin to read.
When you are lonely and you need a friend,
Read the books of Matthew
On Jesus you can depend.
If you are lost and need to be found,
Trust in Jesus—
He'll give you a crown.
Sometimes we feel like no one cares;
Take your burdens to Jesus
And leave them there.
No matter what in life you need, read your Bible
And learn to succeed.
Jesus is just a prayer away.
He's waiting for you
To try Him today.

News Break

Imagine you're reading a newspaper
And this is what you read:
Satan has packed his bags
And from this world has fled.
He left a letter explaining why
He left in a hurry.
Satan wrote that people learned how not to worry.
The letter stated also
That Satan couldn't understand
How people to each other were so kind.
After days of walking to and fro,
He couldn't find
Even one confused mind.
Satan admitted that he was shocked
When all his tools were returned to him
With a note attached that said,
"Leave, Satan, your chances of survival are so slim."
He ran to the phone,
But his hot line was dead.
When Satan saw the demonic spirits leaving,
That's when he fled.
Satan was afraid to roam the streets
When he realized his powers were gone.
He tried to scream for Sin,
But righteousness prevailed.
For once, the world united peacefully
To send Satan back to hell.
The Bible says where there are two or three
Who can touch and agree,
Begin to call on Jesus.
The devil had to flee.
We have God's grace
And His mercy too,
So receive salvation
And he'll make your life brand new.

I'll Rescue Them

Father, prepare my body
That I may go down to Earth
So that man will accept salvation
And his soul will not be cursed.
Father, give me a compassionate heart
to show their needs and concerns,
To let your people know
In hell they don't have to burn.
Was Christ coming in vain?
It seems as though man is content
Doing his own thing.
Now for hell they're bound.

Too Lame

Brainwashed by another man's lie,
I hope they dog you
And make you cry.
Will you forever be so blind,
Skinning and grinning
And licking their behinds?
Prosperity belongs to all mankind,
But you say take it, Mr. Tom,
I don't want mine.
Trading your ideas for a smile,
Tom and his buddies are laughing at you awhile.
You all need your butts beat
'Cause in the end, you're the ones who look cheap.
Little one that can do nothing but giggle—
Why, he don't know.

What Is a Home

Some say a house is a home.
Well, that could be true—
It takes two people sharing and caring.
Honey, that can be me and you.

We've built our relationship
Upon a solid foundation;
We don't want to spoil it
So we'll pray too.

These walls we have filled
With secrecy and pain.
We both know in our lives
We've had sunshine and rain.

Rain, hard and heavy,
But we made it through.
Now let's conquer these problems
Just the Lord, me, and you.

Give Now

The florist sells more flowers
When a person dies
Than they do all year long.
It's sad, many will remember
All the good that one does
Only after one is dead and gone.

Flowers are a symbol
Of what was or should have been said.
So let's start giving them now;
Don't wait until someone is dead.

Sagging Pants

Young man!
Pull those pants up on your waist.
Don't roll your eyes,
And you'd better make haste.
How can you walk
With your pants falling down?
Then you wonder why the cops
Keep coming around.

Underwear showing and
Your butt hanging out;
Tell me, what's that all about?

That isn't a style,
It's more like degrading and looking wild.
Your parents raised you right,
So act like you have good sense—
Get a job and stop hanging
Out on the fence.

Come Together, Let's Pray

Father, we pray for those
Who don't have food to eat.
We pray for those who live under bridges
And are sleeping in the streets.

We come together to pray
For our communities and towns;
We use the authority given to us
So that Satan will be bound.

We pray for our children;
Lord, help us to show concern,
So that in hell
Their souls will not be burned.

We pray for this world that we live in.
We pray that your people
Will return to you again.
As we pray, we look to the hills.
Oh Lord! Hear our cry.
Help us to do your will
On Earth before we die.

Prayer for Mankind

Lord, we come before you today
Seeking guidance about the things
We should and shouldn't say.
Help us to repent
So that we will not continue to live in sin.
We ask that your blessings
Will flow in the lives of all men.
We pray, Lord, as we make this appeal,
That their hearts and minds you will heal.
Some are lost, some are confused,
Some of our men have been abused.
As we stand before the throne of grace,
We ask that men everywhere
Will take their rightful place.

These Women, These Sisters

Lord, these women, you've given us
To walk by our side
Are moving forward;
We men are going along for the ride.

We know that you're leading them on,
Some are powerful and strong.
There is nothing that they can't do—
They are successful in all avenues.
They can take nothing and make a meal,
Their secrets, they will not reveal.
You know what a man will do,
But if you are faithful to a good woman
She will be faithful to you.

How Do You Get From Here To There?

How do you get from here to there?
You make it through fasting and prayer.
You can make it to that home on high
Only if you are willing to give God a try.

You must press on when times are hard,
You must press on when your days are dark.
You have to praise your way through;
It's something that Christ requires of you.

Little Girl

I remember you as a small child;
Today you're here acting disrespectful and wild.
Using profanity too;
I wonder what your parents would do?
You're rolling your eyes and popping your mouth.
I'm calling your parents—better yet—
I'm stopping by your house.

I know you know better than that.
You're only doing this to follow that girl, Pat.
The other children may act this way,
But to you, little girl, I have something to say.

Give me that phone that you are forbidden to have
And again my hand, you'd better not grab.

Where Are You?

Mommy, where are you
When I cry at night for help?
You said you would be there,
But your promises you have not kept.

Where are you
When each day for school
I choose what I should wear?
Granny says you love me,
But why are you never there?

I see other mommies
Holding their little girls' hands.
My eyes are filled with water
And my heart hurts inside.

What's wrong with me, mommy?
Tell me, I'll try to understand.
If it's me that made you mad,
I promise I won't ever be bad.

Each day I set a plate
Before an empty chair.
I get so mad because
You are never there.

I think about the day
I saw those bad men
Come and take you away.

Each night I pray for you.
I hear Grandmama crying too.
Mommy, do you love me?
I want you to just come home
So that we can be together again.
Mommy, it's where you belong.

Where are you? What is it you do
That keeps us apart?
I miss you and I love you.
This is really hard.

Adams' Chapel

This church started
From services held in a tent.
A preacher came to town shouting, "Repent!"
The Adams were as the woman
That gave the prophet room to preach.
It was through their obedience
Plenty of souls were reached.

Their home was anointed
And known as Holy ground;
The spirit was high
And Satan was bound.
Later they were directed
To build a church on the hill.
It was small, but they were willing to do God's will.

People came from miles around.
Once the doors opened,
Not an empty seat could be found.
The theme was "Give Me The Word."
It was during those days, the Gospel was heard.

The older faithful warriors
Have gone on to rest.
They were a band of believers
Who were truly blessed.

Mother Heath

This elderly woman started a long time ago
Faithfully planting her seeds;
And she had a chance
To watch them grow.
Parents place their children
Willingly in her care.
They weren't afraid,
They saw the spirit
Of Christ dwelling there.
She carried a street full of children
Up and down the road.
In her hand she had a "switch" that let them know,
"Peace was aboard!"
This was a church mother
Who loved to praise God;
Doing things to help the church.
For her, was never hard.
She made us young people
Gather at the alter to pray;
Just call on Jesus
Was what she encouraged us to say.
"Do, Lord, Remember Me"
Was her favorite song.
She plowed her rows to the end
Until it all was done.
Sleep on, Mother Heath,
You must enjoy your rest
We all loved you,
But God loved you best.

Real Talk

I know I had walked away
From the teaching I received as a child.
However, I never thought my life
Would end up being crazy and foul.
I wanted to leave home
To be my own boss;
Now my parents are shamed of me
And the friends I chose are false.
I didn't understand how so quickly
I went from up to down.
I knew my parents raised me right;
I never intended to sleep around.
This man I gave my body to
Treated me harsh and mean.
He often backhanded me across the face
Then dared me to scream.
At first I drank liquor followed by the pills;
One day I was on the corners
Begging for my meals.
I no longer held my head up in the air;
I was just like a bum
And no one had time to spare.
I ate food that was thrown in the garbage can;
Onlookers shook their heads in disgust,
But not one would lend a hand.
So for all of you teenagers
Chasing behind what you call your man,
Better rethink this and stay home as long as you can.
You think you can't wait to be your own boss.
Tell me, how many of you
Can afford to pay the cost?

Looking for Jesus in All the Wrong Places

If you are looking for Jesus
In that bottle of booze,
Let me tell you this,
You're terribly confused.
If you thought he was on the ballroom floor,
Make up your minds,
Don't go there no more.
Jesus has never been
In any of those places.
He travelled the land
And comforted many faces.
He's standing with His arms opened wide;
It's in your heart that He wants to abide.
Jesus wasn't in that fight
You had at home.
Parents, He's not pleased
When you stay out all night long.
He wasn't in that lie
You say you had to tell.
It's things like that
That will send your soul to hell.
Some people like to refer to Jesus
As being a spare;
Maybe you ought to check to see
If He is still there.

"Thank You, Mom"

You'll never know
How much I thank you
For your support
And kindness each day through.
This gift isn't much
Of a gift at all;
It's the thought that counts
In situations great and small.
You were there no matter when.
It's not over yet (smile);
I may need you again.

Take a Look in the Book and See If My Name Is There

If reservations were made at the airport,
Once you've reached the desk,
You stand before the clerk
To confirm the request.
I'd like to know the time of my departure
And when I'm due back;
Take a look in the book
And see if my name is there.
Maybe you went to a restaurant
Where reservations were made.
Others had to wait,
But for you and your guest special seats were saved.
All the hostess had to do was take a look in the book
To confirm the name is you.
Some folks will join the church
To get names on the roll,
And before their One Year Anniversary
What stories can be told!
You saw them more in the streets
Than you did in the pews;
Some of them led such double lives
They made the evening news.
Some people in the church don't even pay their tithes,
Wont give to the poor or give their neighbors a ride.
Some folks seem to think fortune and fame
Will get them there.
Others think they can make it
On a wing and a prayer.
Now is a time to make it right
So that you can enjoy the sights.
For each of our lives, Jesus does care.

In the *Book of Life* he wants
All of our names to be there.
Be faithful in all that you do
So you won't hear the words,
"Depart, I never knew you."

Do the Right Thing

Train up a child in the way they should go
So that when they're grown they will know
How to act like a man,
Learn how to be a provider,
How to work with his own hands.
You can't train them if you aren't there.
They need to know, for them you care.
Abusive language doesn't help a child;
It only makes them harsh and wild.
Spare the rod, spoil the child;
It's your job as parents
To teach them how to walk a mile.
Respect is something
That should be taught at home,
The teachers can't do it alone.
Teach your child
How to take care of their own needs;
And for God's sake, teach them to read.
Some parents are sitting back
Not saying or doing a thing
While losing their children
To drugs and gangs.

Life

What is life?
Life is living—
Living is giving
Each and every day.

The things you treasure the most—
Nothing you want to throw away.
Life is more precious
Than silver and gold,
Yet it is often taken for granted
By both young and old.

Life is a crossbreed
Of happiness and sorrow.
One may face disappointment today
But rejoice on tomorrow.

Life is a challenge
As well as a chance.
Either you remain in tradition
Or progress forward and advance.

Life is for us
What Jesus gave;
He died, that we might be saved.

Fight On

Don't let no one shake your faith,
You qualify to run in this race.
Hold on and believe there is hope.
When challenges occur,
Learn how to cope.

Positive attitudes are what we need.
Things can be better,
So let's take heed.

We are somebody as we all know,
And we deserve more than just a job to go.

We need benefits.
We need to stand
And give the boss
A list of our demands.

Educate Your Own Child

Many of our young people
Are going astray
Because many parents aren't examples
Leading the way.
Some will and some wont succeed
Due to the fact
That they are unable to read.
Some of them won't attend school long—
Some are too old
And their motives are wrong.
Educate your own child;
Don't wait until they are wild.
Deal with them while they are young;
Teach them to put a bridle on their tongue.
Teach them respect too—
Don't allow them to disrespect their elders;
Don't allow them to disrespect you.
Teach them how in life
To work with their own hands.
Fathers, it's your job
To teach the boys
How to be men.
Teach them to have hopes and dreams;
Get them off the streets
With drug dealers and their schemes.

But who's going to teach them if you are not there?
Some think it was a heated moment and you had no time to spare.
Now it's the mother's job to do both;
But after the job is done, the dad will boast the most.
Educate your girls; they need to stay in school.
Encourage them to have self-respect, for them, set some home-rules.
A young lady should carry herself with grace and

She shouldn't walk around with bruises on her face (that came from a man).
Her mouth shouldn't be filthy and foul;
She can't run with a man.
She's not built that way.
Teach her to cook for her own children;
Teach her how to pray.
But who's going to teach her if, by chance, you aren't there?
Who's going to teach them, parents, when neither of you are at home?
How can they learn from you
When you're both out there doing wrong?

Mama and Daddy are both in jail,
Or daddy walked out a long time ago.
Said he needed space.
Where he went, no one knows.
Mama met her a new man who doesn't work;
Just sits home and makes demands.
How and what will the children learn?
How to be on welfare
Or how to be bums all the time?
Educate your child
Before they start committing crimes.
Or is it too late?
They already made the mistake.

All in Your Smile

Each time I see you
I'm greeted with a smile;
It gives me the assurance
That I can go that extra mile.

The words spoken
Are gentle and true;
This is my way of saying
I appreciate you.

You've never talked much,
As I recall,
But the smile you wear
Tells it all.

There may be in your body
Aches and pains,
But the expressions I've noticed
Remain the same.

Keep on keeping on
With that beautiful smile;
It blesses others,
For it helps them go that extra mile.

You will always be remembered
As the lady with the smiling face.

Watch Yourself

Watch yourself and your household too;
Mind your own business.
This is nothing new.

When it comes down to others,
We don't care what we say or do.
Have you looked in the mirror lately
To see your faults staring back at you?

Watch yourself and your lies too;
God has a record that is kept on you.
"Judge not" is what the Bible says.
It states other things to help you
In many other ways.

Watch as well as pray, this is true,
But watch yourself
No matter what you do.

Happy Birthday

I've noticed your hair
On your head is gray;
you're missing a tooth or two.
Go to the dentist
He'll know what to do.
He will guarantee you a spare,
But let the beautician dye your hair.

Folks are saying
your mind is bad too.
Child, you're a wreck,
what good is left of you?
Now, all of this
Was just a joke;
Quit looking pale
Like you want to croak.

Happy Birthday!

Mess

Mess on the left,
Mess on the right,
Mess in the front, mess in the back.
Mess in the center
And on the corners too,
Mess on the sidewalk—
How can you get through?
You stepped over mess,
You passed by mess,
And mess is hindering you
From getting your rest.
Mess on the job,
Mess at home, something has to give,
Mess just needs to be gone.
The house is a mess,
The car is a mess,
You're a mess,
And you need to rest.
Get out of here
'Cause mess is stuck under the bottom of your feet.
I suggest we have a funeral to bury mess.
One can wear a suit and the other can wear a dress.
The eulogy can be, "We grew weary of mess; therefore,
We are gathered here today at the people's request
To say farewell and to bury mess.
Our burdens are light just knowing you are gone.
Don't try to call; there are blocks on our phones."

In My House

Rules and regulations
Are established in this house.
These rules were made
By me and my spouse.

You are expected to follow
And carry them through;
The day that you don't
Will be me, him, then you.

You all aren't babies
And we won't treat you that way,
But you aren't grown either,
So you better watch what you say.

Don't try to leave,
'Cause you have no where to go,
And the day you try to cross me,
I'll knock you through the floor.
Why?
Because you're in my house.

Children Abused by Parents

It's not right for children
To be slapped around
Because no job for the parent
Can be found.

You wanted so badly
To leave home,
Stating you couldn't wait
Until you were grown.

The only time
You feel like a man
Is when you are using
The back of your hand.

Slapping and knocking
Those innocent children around—
They ought to gain courage
And give you a good beat down.

Abuse

Dial 1-800-See-If-I-Care;
You had nothing to give,
So it's no love lost there.

You demanded this and that,
One thing or another.
You didn't treat me
Like a lover.

You did me wrong;
You treated me bad.
Now that it's over,
I am glad.

The pain in my heart
I hope some day will heal;
Get help, people,
Because abuse is real.
(Coming the heart of a hurting man.)

Abuse Hurts

You picked me up
To pull me down.
When you saw my smile,
You quickly changed it
To a frown.

You told lies to discredit me;
You kept me bound,
Didn't want me free.
You brought me to an open shame,
Always scandalizing my name.

I was afraid in public
To show my face
Because you said
I was a disgrace.

You beat me down
With your mouth.
I thought you loved me
As your spouse.

But I see I was wrong.

Go Fast

Go fast!
Everything on the highway
I want you to pass.
It's somebody else's car so why can't you just
Go fast!
Let your friends see
How fast I can run.

We got all the time in the world
And we're just having a little fun.

Go fast!
Scare that old lady
As she walks across the street.

Go fast!
The light is yellow
I know you got it beat.

Go fast!
You can outrun the cop.

Go fast!
Don't you stop.
Finally a train is across the track.
Hey man, what are you doing?
You've got to pull back—

Bam! In a hurry preparing to die.

"Everyone in the vehicle is dead"
Is what the headlines in the newspapers read.
Now six young men, all dead and gone.
None had driver's licenses,
And the driver was in the wrong.
They were clocked doing 122
Drugs were found in their bodies … and alcohol too.

Drama Queen

The drama queen wants to be seen
Because she thinks her game is mean.
But whenever she comes around,
She thinks she brings others down.
Yet when they see her coming
They laugh instead of frown.

The latest gossip
She strives to tell all.
Everyone talking 'bout how she wears her garments
two sizes too small.

Whenever things aren't going her way,
She starts with the drama
About having such a bad day.

She has so many disguises,
You don't know which one is real.
She is so dramatic
She can't even be still.

The drama queen eats food filled with hate.
She always shows up at events
An hour late,
Only to be seen.
Don't forget … she's the *drama queen*!

A Virtuous Woman of God

Her hair is whiter than snow;
From her mouth, wisdom flows.
She's a precious jewel
That comes without a price.
She's the church mother
Who gives good advice.

She is humble in her spirit,
Always praying that young mothers
Will lead a productive life,
That they will bring their children to church
And stop living before them
Sinful lives filled with strife.

She prays that young men
Will leave the violence alone
And return to church
To learn how in Christ
They can be strong.

You see her sitting
On the pew wearing a smile.
She is a watchman on the wall,
Praying all the while.

She prays for the pastor
As before the congregation
He stands to preach.
She prays for the choir
That through their songs
Souls can be reached.

She prays that all
Will see the light.
She prays that the life she lives
Is pleasing in God's sight.

Christians, Stop Praising the Devil

Satan is the prince of the air;
It's his job to cause destruction everywhere.
He is a thief, liar, and hypocrite.
It's his job to tear down;
He's not going to quit.

He's walking daily
To and fro,
Seeking those that say
They can't take it anymore.

He was thrown out of heaven
So long ago,
But this he doesn't
Want you to know.

He is the prince of the air,
But none of your burden
Will he help you to bear.

All he wants to do
Is to be invited in.
He comes with help
To keep you in sin.

He rejoices when in church his name is called.
He rejoices when about him we tell it all.

But, Christians, you don't need
To give him any praise.
If you resist the devil,
He has to flee.
Believe Christ died to set you free.

That Young Lady Did Well

That young lady wasn't slack.
She made something of herself;
She didn't fall through the crack.
She too came from a broken home;
Most of the time, both of her parents were gone.

But she always stayed in her schoolbooks;
She wasn't concerned or pressured about looks.
She worked hard to get ahead.
Once she made it,
This is how the article read:
"She's the Speaker of the House,
She's the Secretary of State,
With morals and values she held on to.
That young lady, in life, did great.
She never caused her parents
to walk in shame.
She worked diligently
To give herself a good name."

Thank You, Mom

Thank you, Mom,
For the roads you've paved,
And for the sacrifices for us you made.

You taught us how to go to the Lord in prayer,
And for each other to care.
It's those prayers
That are carrying us on today.

"Lord, bless my little ones;
Watch over them through the night.
Even when they are disobedient,
Be their guiding light."

You worked hard
Even when you were sick.
It was your determination not to quit.

And then it happened—you died.
Our hearts were in shock.
There were times when our days were dark.

Thank God for the memories
We can and do many times share.
Mom you're in our hearts;
You will always be there.

A Gamble Moment of Truth

Everybody wants a good spouse.
Do you have what it takes to
Keep them satisfied at your house?
Some of our behaviors are
So low-down mean,
They kill all hopes and destroy chances for
Fulfilling our dreams.
Some couples are anxious
To jump in and out of bed;
No talk about the future,
They just want their sexual desires fed.
Some woman with an ugly attitude
Is seeking a tall, handsome man
When what she really needs
Is an attitude-adjustment plan.
Some don't like loneliness,
So they settle for anything,
And then after shacking together
For over twenty years wonder why
They can't get a ring.
Others try to justify their actions
As to why they never said I do,
When the truth of the matter is,
How can you marry someone
That has never asked you to?

God's Glory

Each morning God
Commands his beauty
To cover Earth.
Sunrise! Step forward,
Sunrise! Give birth!

To see this happen
Means darkness
Has faded away.
You have the power
To speak and command your day.

You can command your mornings
To be sunny and bright.
You can declare and decree
Your children will do right.

You can pray for wisdom
So that your finances change.
If you believe you can,
You can have these things.

You have the power to speak
Life or death,
Poverty or wealth,
Sickness or good health.
They lie within
The power of your tongue.
Start exercising faith
So that your victories can be won.

The moon,
God's glory before us, shines so bright;
The stars portray a picture of heaven
As a powerful sight.

The clouds
Are angels sailing
Through the sky,
Waiting for God
To give them charge
To minister to you and I.

The rain
Sheds drops of victory,
Reminding us that
God has it all under control.
He wants us to listen to his voice
As he speaks to our souls.

The rainbow's
The agreement
Between God and man;
The skies show
Signs and wonders
That time is at hand.

*P*recious

Be strong!
It's okay.
We know your hearts
Were saddened on the day
When from you we were all taken away.
I promised my classmates
I would let their families know.
Things happened so rapidly and
We had to go.
Just know that we never
Felt any pain.
Our bodies were transformed.
What we did experience
Was a supernatural change!

An angel appeared before us
Covering twenty small bodies
Under her powerful wings.
It was at that moment we saw
So many wonderful things,
The girls described the wings as
Soft and warm protective shields.
The boys begged the differ; they said,
"The wings were made of steel!"

After we were gathered up together,
We were taken to this place
Where the atmosphere was peaceful.
It was filled with love and grace.
We were all instructed
To go into this room
That had designs of rainbows and
Colorful balloons.

The scenery was such a heavenly sight:
There were little angels ministering
All dressed in white.
Don't be angry, please!
Don't be sad.
We were grateful for the wonderful years
We shared with our moms and dads.
When your hearts are heavy and the tears you cry
Are filled with pain, remember,
There is strength in Jesus's name.

Note from the author:
The next several pages are honoring the little ones as well as the teachers at Sandy Hook Elementary School in Newtown, Connecticut. I pause for a moment of silence to honor the families that suffered a great loss. My thoughts and prayers are with you. Just know that the world grieves with you. Words will never replace the loss you've suffered, but your loved ones will never be forgotten by the world.

Our parents are extremely sad.
Dad blames Mom and Mom blames Dad.
They look at each other
With hurt on their faces,
Both wishing with their child they could exchange places.
We were taken away as a group
That is now instrumental in playing
Harps and flutes.

Our day begins and ends
With us sitting at Jesus's feet.
His voice sounds like
Running water that's powerful
Yet gentle and sweet.

You remember us as being young and small;
That's not the way we are viewed up here at all.
We are sent forth all over the world
To bring in the souls of little boys and girls.

Heaven is filled with joy and delight,
Where hearts are pure and spirits are bright.
We were taken from earth before
Our hearts were tainted or even stained.
We are spiritual angels
That have been changed.
Whenever you feel lonely, please don't cry.
We are on an assignment. Just know that God
Has us all together in His mansion on high.

Injustice

Remembering
Mr. Trayvon Martin

An innocent and jovial teen,
His life ended without a chance
To pursue his dreams.
To his family he never
Got to say goodbye.
Why
Did this young black teen
On that night have to die?
He went to the store to buy some treats
And was gunned down
Like an animal in the streets.
The killer was a wannabe cop
Who called 9-1-1,
Yet, he fired the first shot.
The operator instructed him
In his vehicle to stay,
But he disobeyed and
Followed this young man anyway.
Trayvon Martin died without a cause.
The courts acquitted the killer
By using some bogus laws.
This young man died without a clue;
Trayvon could have been
Either me or you.
Justice is sought,
Fairness is right,
A beloved one's life
Was taken that night.
How could the officials use his parents
To appeal to the public

To demonstrate peace
When
No justice was rendered
For their son who's deceased?

In loving memory of Mr. Trayvon Martin.

written
July 31, 2013

Goodbye, My Love

The days of my life
Have come to an end.
Only God can determine
Whether I lost
Or
If I did win.

The truth
Is greater than anything.
You and others will see,
It was about me, my past,
And my life's history.

Maybe I'll be remembered
For troubled times.
People tend to hold wicked
Memories in their minds.
Perhaps
After many refrain
From throwing stones,
They'll recall
I asked for forgiveness
For all my wrongs.

My fans thought
I possessed so much,
When I simply wanted
To be loved and touched.

I was looking
For a chance
To be accepted for me,
Not just my songs and dance.
There was a shy
Woman begging to be free
From the demons that
Had a stronghold on me.
Thank you
For believing in me.
From the turmoil of life,
I've been set free.

Thank you, and
Goodbye, my love.
You were the ones
That wore the golden gloves.
In loving memory
Of
Whitney Houston
Known for the number-one hit
"The Greatest Love of All"

written
February 13, 2012

The Godfather of Soul

Dance moves and music
Wouldn't be as successful
As they are today if
In the music industry
This man didn't pave the way.
He broke down barriers
That carried a stronghold.
I am speaking of none other than
The Godfather of Soul.
He was a legend of his kind;
His music was heartfelt and genuine.
The hardest-working man in show business.
There are many fans and associates
That to this can be a witness.
His trademark was the slide and the split,
And when the cape was draped around his shoulders,
You could barely sit.
Fans screamed and cried with tears of joy.
At Christmas he gave away turkeys and
To the tots, he gave away toys.
Mr. James Brown had a heart of gold.
Maybe that's why he was called
The Godfather of Soul.

About the Author

I am the composer of this collection of poems with the exception of one poem that was written by myself and my sister, Bernese, in memory of our mother, Mrs. Della M. Rawls Hines.

I believe that each of us is blessed with a unique gift. It's up to the individual to allow it to spring forth and blossom. Gifts are talents that are to be shared with others. In sharing them, others can and will receive comfort, strength, love, and encouragement.

As you read my poetry, I pray that it will take you to levels unknown in your life that will help you to be all that you can be in Christ. When you read the poems, I know there will be laughter, tears, oohs, and aahs, and "I know she didn't go there." Yes, I did, for it needed to be said.

I pray that you will share these poems in your churches, homes, and schools and wherever there is a need. Be blessed and look for my second book, coming soon.

About the book

For all of my readers who enjoyed my first book of poetry, I am about to give birth: I have another book coming soon. I carried them for many months; now they are long overdue. That's why I will be sharing them with you.

Take them to church, read them at home; apply them to your lives and you won't go wrong. Some of my poems are filled with laughter; some illustrate pain. Some tell what happens when one calls on Jesus's name.

I need you, once again, to take this ride with me. I promise it will be adventurous, and you'll want to have faith.

From the Author of *Dat Ain't All*.